This book belongs to

_ _ _ _ _ _ _ _ _ _ _ _ _ _

CURIOSITY

CONNECTION

CREATION

Collection

Creative Ninja

By Mary Nhin

I was working on a new project when Focused Ninja walked in.

Focused Ninja took out a small notebook. In it, there was a colorful circle.

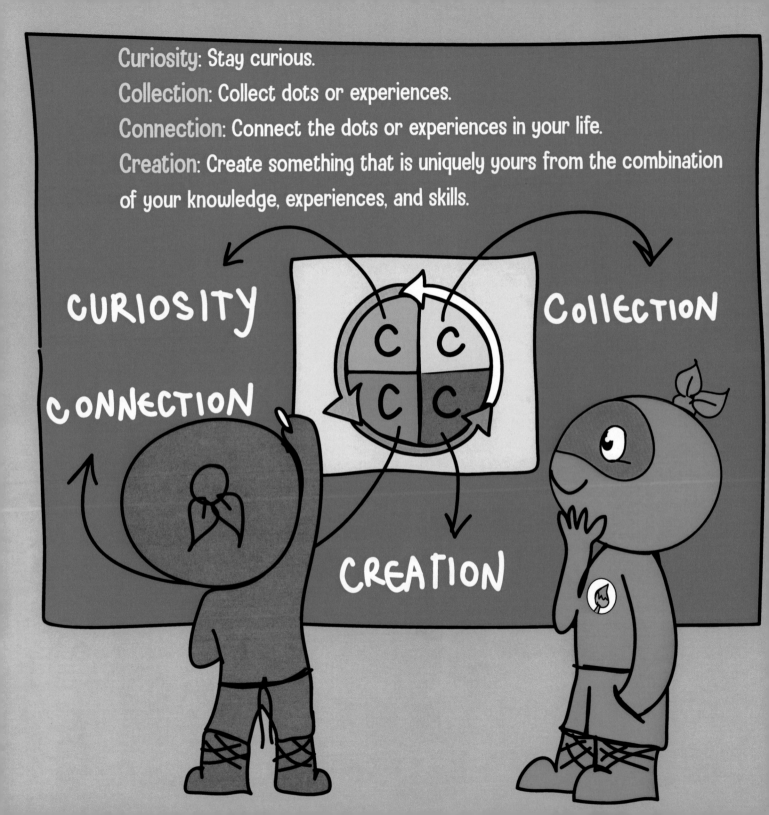

Curiosity means a strong desire to know or learn something.

Here are some ways I stay curious:

It is great to experience new things! Here's a rough sketch of my collection of experiences:

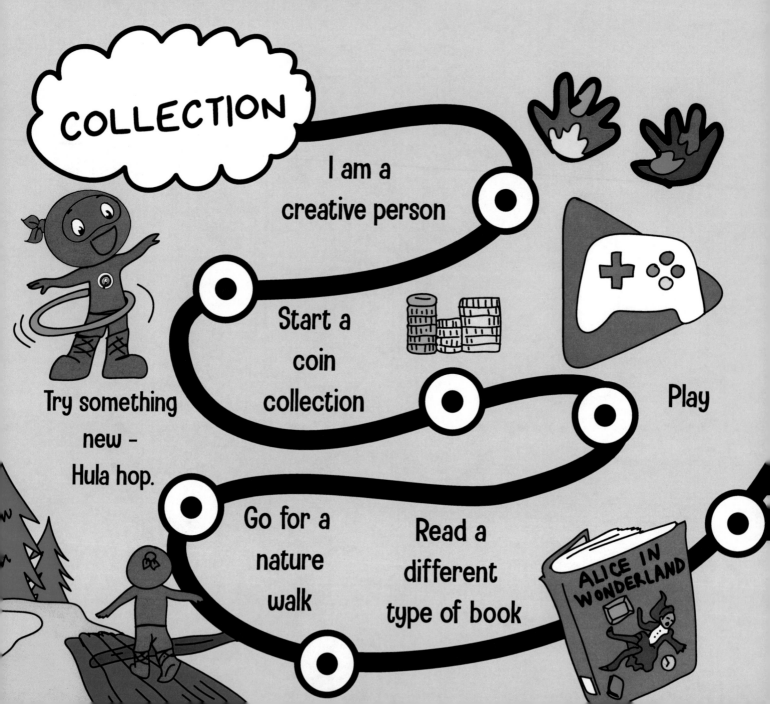

COLLECTION

I am a creative person

Try something new - Hula hop.

Start a coin collection

Play

Go for a nature walk

Read a different type of book

ALICE IN WONDERLAND

Connection happens when you connect the dots or experiences in your life together somehow. It usually involves a lot of thinking, imagination, and maybe even some boredom.

For example, in art class the other day, I was thinking about what to draw. Mrs. Johnson said we could draw anything we wanted. I thought about how I loved visiting the National Yellowstone Park last year, and then I thought about what we learned when we mix primary colors together. I asked myself, "How could I connect those two?"

Creation happens when you create something that is uniquely yours from the combination of your knowledge, experiences, and skills.

...which added to my collection of experiences and knowledge.

Then, I connected some of my experiences. For example, in reading class, we just learned about how to retell a story.

And since Mrs Johnson wanted us to do something turkey related...

I created this turkey story telling hand!

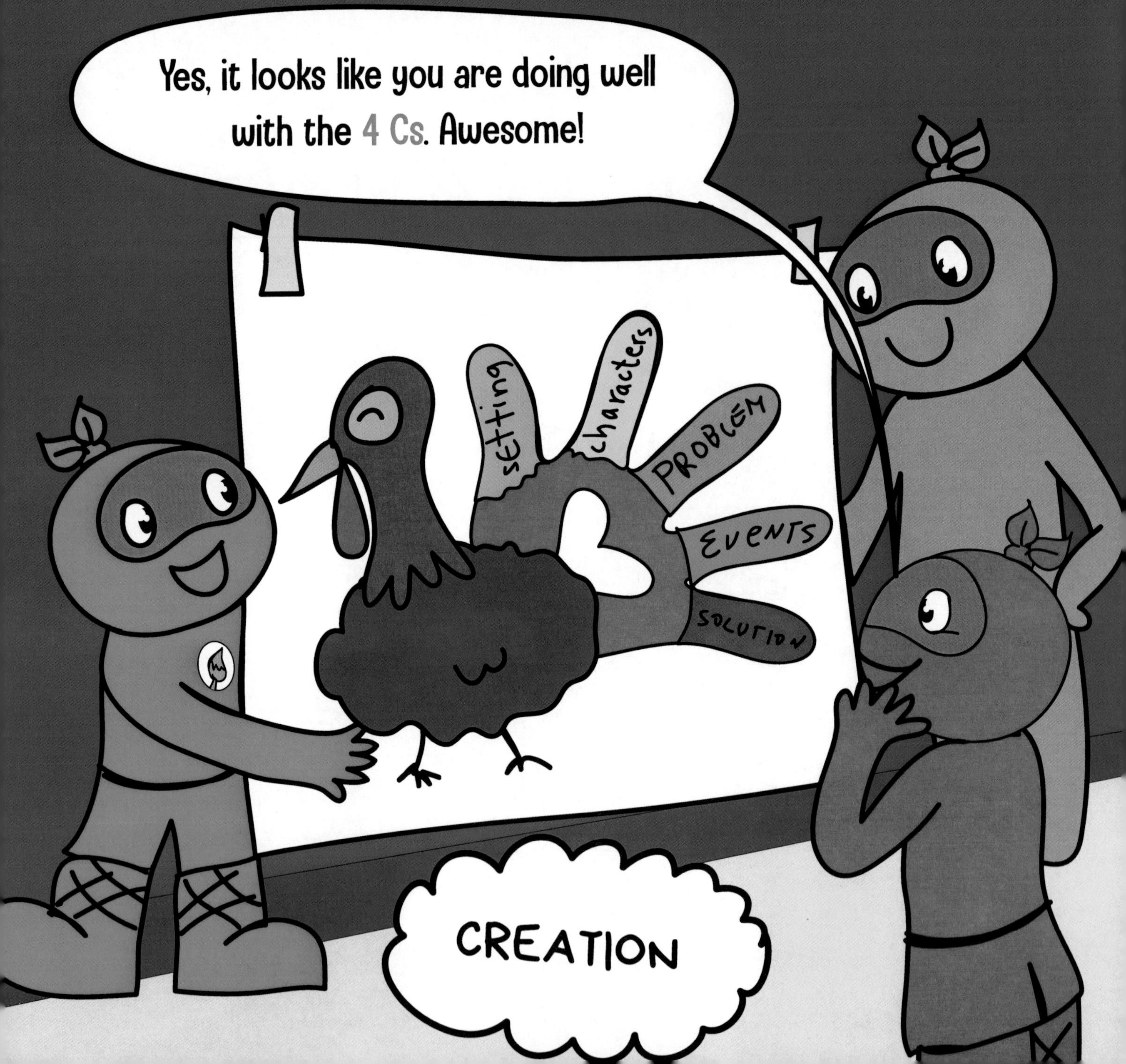

I nodded happily.

It really does work!

Made in United States
North Haven, CT
16 December 2021

13052144R00020